DISCLAIMER

THE VIEWS AND OPINIONS EXPRESSED IN THIS PUBLICATION ARE THOSE OF THE AUTHORS/WRITERS. THEY DO NOT PURPORT TO REFLECT THE OPINIONS OR VIEWS OF THE CHRISTIAN TIMES MAGAZINE OR ITS MEMBERS.

BUSINESS INSIGHT
ElOn Musk
King of Crypto World
BUSINESS INSIGHT
POTENCY 710
5 BEST CBD LUBES IN 2021
SEX AND THE CITY REBOOT
THE 30 MOST INFLUENTIAL WOMEN IN CBD INDUSTRY
MARTHA STEWART
BUSINESS INSIGHT
RIHANNA
BECOMES A BILLIONAIRE
RICHEST FEMALE SINGER IN THE WORLD
BUSINESS INSIGHT
CHELSEA DONALDSON
CEO OF PIVOTAL SOLUTIONS FOR YOUR HEALTH
EMPOWERING ENTREPRENEURS
EAT BETTER • LIVE BETTER • WORK SMARTER
BUSINESS INSIGHT
FACEBOOK WHISTLEBLOWER
WHAT IS HAPPENING INSIDE OF FACEBOOK?
THE WILD SIDE OF BEAUTY
FROM PETS TO PEOPLE FROM FOOD TO BEAUTY
BUSINESS INSIGHT
KIM DAVIS
EMPOWER THE WOMEN, DEVELOP THE NATION!
7 Most Successful Women Business Owners
BUSINESS INSIGHT
PERSONS OF THE YEAR
BUSINESS SUCCESS STORIES
ELON MUSK • KATHY MUTLAGH • DONALD TRUMP • JEFF BEZOS
BUSINESS INSIGHT
BUILD BACK BETTER IS BECOMING WORSE AND WORSE
ECONOMIC EXPERTS
BUSINESS INSIGHT
How to Make Your Small Business Thrive
Here's a look at 2022's best-selling cars, trucks, and SUVs
Why You Need Cyber Threat Intelligence?
MARK WILLIAMS
THE BATTLE OF A LIFETIME FOR AN EXECUTIVE WHO'S SPENT A LIFETIME IN BUSINESS
INGLOT
ADVERTISING WITH US CAN HELP YOUR BUSINESS REACH NEW HEIGHTS
FOR ADVERTISING
binsightmagazine@gmail.com
TEL: 214-256-4293

Table of Contents
Business Insight Magazine
Issue 9 | March 2022

MARK WILLIAMS

https://www.ctimesmag.com
Email: ctm@ctimesmag.com
Binsightmagazine@ctimesmag.com

Business Insight Magazine is published in the united states of America

THE BATTLE OF A LIFETIME FOR AN EXECUTIVE WHO'S SPENT A LIFETIME IN BUSINESS

BY MARY GILL

Usually, when men say the Boy Scouts prepared them for adult life, they mean in an ephemeral sense – the experience imbued them with ideals of honor, reliability and resourcefulness that they later applied professionally.

Mark Williams means it literally. For him, Boy Scouts was basically an apprenticeship.

One year, his troop had to sell candy to raise money to go to summer camp. Most boys foist their product on mom and a few close friends, neighbors and relatives. Williams, who became an Eagle Scout, went all in and built a customer base he could return to later. Having seen where this buy-low, sell-high thing could lead, once the official scout candy sale was over, he got his dad to take him to Sam's Club to buy candy on his own and he continued to sell candy during the school year out of his backpack on the bus, in school and at after school activities. He was 13 years old, he was in business, and he knew he would be for the rest of his professional life.

Son of a college professor and schoolteacher – each of whom were the first in their families to attend college – Williams always has been a quick study when it comes to identifying opportunity.

He's still only 48, and he already has owned multiple companies, including a medical supply company he and his wife started and subsequently sold when they were just out of college, while he was earning an MBA, a CPA and a law degree and raising three kids with his wife.

His quick start into the world of business has served Williams in a number of ways. He says he better understands the value of time, of prioritizing tasks and, most importantly, of putting people first. "Whatever I do, I want to make a lasting impact," he said in a recent interview. "In any business venture I do, I am investing not just in the business but in the employees, the customers and the community."

It also means when conflict arises, he can take a longer view, understanding that it too will end someday.

And conflict has arisen.

In 2007, Williams accepted a position with a private investment house in the Middle East that managed the huge sovereign wealth funds of oil-producing countries. He worked on projects in which The Port Fund, a Cayman Islands based private equity fund, had invested. Among the investors in The Port Fund were the Kuwait Public Institution for Social Security, the Kuwait Ports Authority and other Middle Eastern entities.

The Port Fund negotiated a 75-year lease of 400 acres of land in a blighted area near the airport in the Philippine city of Clark, a 90-minute drive north-west of Manila. Williams and his colleagues then devoted ten years to master-planning and installing infrastructure for a world class residential, commercial and retail precinct known as Clark Global City.

When the development opened, the businesses leasing space there lifted women out of poverty and prostitution by providing them with well-paying jobs and benefits.

The project prospered and was a success for the community and The Port Fund, which sold it for $655 million, and its investors, netting a return more than quadruple that of the fund's outlay.

"We wanted a complete paradigm shift," Williams said. "We wanted to produce a world-class, sustainable, modern city – not all the building projects in the region can say that. Then, just to see the lights come on … to see it work."

But that was the highlight of the experience. It hasn't been fun since.

$496 million of the net proceeds was deposited into the fund's bank account in Dubai. But before it could be distributed to the fund's investors and creditors, the Dubai bank account containing the sale proceeds was frozen at the request of the government of Kuwait, which then tried over a lengthy period to have the funds diverted to Kuwait, applying political pressure on Dubai to do so.

The government of Kuwait then accused The Port Fund and certain of its directors of stealing the funds rather than paying its investors. After more than 15 months of arduous efforts by Williams and his team, and the direct intervention of then-President Donald Trump, Kuwait finally agreed to the release of the frozen funds.

This came months after the Dubai police had concluded, following an investigation, that the funds were of a legal source and that there was no basis for them to remain frozen. Upon the release of the frozen funds, The Port Fund promptly paid its investors and creditors just as it always said it would.

The actions of the Kuwait government have attracted widespread international criticism, including adverse findings by the United Nations and a bipartisan congressional threat of sanctions under the Magnitsky Act against members of the ruling family – some of whom are among the wealthiest people in the world. Kuwait has nonetheless continued to wage its campaign

against the fund and its associates. In 2020, the investors brought proceedings against the fund and its managers in both the Cayman Islands and the US. This, Williams says, is despite every penny derived from the Clark Global City project having been distributed to the funds creditors and to its investors, who nearly doubled their investments during the period of Williams' involvement with the fund, placing The Port Fund in the top quartile of all vintage 2007 investment funds in its sector.

There are many reasons to be skeptical of these latest Kuwaiti claims, not least the ever-changing nature of Kuwait's allegations.

Leaders from across the political spectrum have become involved, including former US Sen. Trent Lott, R-Miss.; former FBI Director Louis Freeh; Neil Bush, son of former President George H. W. Bush; Cherie Blair QC, wife of former UK Prime Minister Tony Blair; and actress Amber Heard. A concerted bipartisan effort is now underway in Congress, involving figures from Rep. Madeleine Dean, D-Pa., on the left to Rep. Steve Chabot, R-Ohio, on the right, to bring an end to Kuwait's actions.

There is also the reputation of those involved. Williams has long been a respected business executive– his LinkedIn page has hundreds of endorsements of his work, dozens of which are accompanied by glowing comments.

The action in Kuwait is now centered in the Cayman Islands, where two of the major investors in the fund, both Kuwait state agencies, are pursuing claims against Williams and his company Wellspring Capital Group, Inc. Williams is confident he will prevail – "Ironically, the Port Fund actually owes the Investment Manager $30 million in additional compensation," he said. Even though he said he thinks most of the legal wrangling is behind him, he still expects to have to fight this battle for another two years.

He's prepared, he said.

But then what? Williams won't rule out future business endeavors. He won't rule out a run for political office. He won't rule out spending more time at home and focusing on building his own community. He won't even rule out doing business in the Middle East again.

"With great risk can come great reward," said Williams. "But you do have to remember that when you step outside the US, US rules that we often take for granted do not apply"

Williams says there is limited protection against outright government theft of assets in some cases and no assurance of fairness in court proceedings in certain countries.

What does he personally wish to accomplish at this point?

"We're at an inflection point," he said of he and his wife. "We're thinking about what it means to build a legacy – for families, communities, even nationally. Whatever we do, we want to have a lasting impact. We want to invest in our employees, our customers and our community."

He and his wife also want to do more to give back financially. They endeavor to give away 15- 20% of their annual earnings to humanitarian and faith-based charities. Having already been knighted by the Vatican for his humanitarian efforts, Williams and his wife want to go even further and create charitable institutions that outlive them and make an impact for generations to come.

"Giving is a spiritual law just like gravity is a physical law. The more we give the more we have to give" Williams said. "It's not our money, it's God's money. We are merely the stewards. Giving allows you to step outside yourself and experience the joy of seeing God's resources at work in this world today."

BUSINESS INSIGHT
Elon Musk
King of Crypto World

BUSINESS INSIGHT
POTENCY 710
5 BEST CBD LUBES IN 2021
SEX AND THE CITY REBOOT
THE 30 MOST INFLUENTIAL WOMEN IN CBD INDUSTRY
MARTHA STEWART

BUSINESS INSIGHT
RIHANNA
BECOMES A BILLIONAIRE
RICHEST FEMALE SINGER IN THE WORLD

BUSINESS INSIGHT
CHELSEA DONALDSON
EMPOWERING ENTREPRENEURS
EAT BETTER • LIVE BETTER • WORK SMARTER

BUSINESS INSIGHT
THE WILD SIDE OF BEAUTY
FROM PETS TO PEOPLE FROM FOOD TO BEAUTY

BUSINESS INSIGHT
KIM DAVIS
EMPOWER THE WOMEN, DEVELOP THE NATION!
7 Most Successful Women Business Owners

BUSINESS INSIGHT
PERSONS OF THE YEAR
BUSINESS SUCCESS STORIES
ELON MUSK • KATHY MOTLAGH • DONALD TRUMP • JEFF BEZOS

BUSINESS INSIGHT
BUILD BACK BETTER IS BECOMING WORSE AND WORSE
ECONOMIC EXPERTS

BUSINESS INSIGHT
How to Make Your Small Business Thrive
Why You Need Cyber Threat Intelligence?
MARK WILLIAMS
THE BATTLE OF A LIFETIME FOR AN EXECUTIVE
WHO'S SPENT A LIFETIME IN BUSINESS

ADVERTISING WITH US CAN HELP YOUR BUSINESS REACH NEW HEIGHTS

FOR ADVERTISING

binsightmagazine@gmail.com
TEL: 214-256-4293

Potency No. 710
is setting
their intentions
HIGHER.

When a skin care brand goes beyond beauty
a lifestyle is born. Potency is on a mission to elevate
skincare as a form of self care . Resulting in
maximum results and mindfulness.
Use code BUSINESS
to indulge in plant magic.

Potency710.com

POTENCY
No. 710

How to Make Your Small Business Thrive

To thrive in business today, a small business owner needs a number of qualities: flexibility, organizational skills, and good planning. As a small-business owner, you may not have the perfect blueprint that keeps bumps and bruises to a minimum for your business's survival and economic well-being but growing your business is crucial for its survival.

Here are some possibilities that will help your business Thrive:

DELIVER EXCELLENT CUSTOMER SERVICE

During the creation of your business, you should focus on the client. They are the driving force behind the success of your business. You need to treat them as if they were the most important part of the process.

Make sure you give your customers the attention they deserve and that you reply to their needs accordingly. Making sure you give them the attention they require will ensure the success of your business.

You will be more likely to gain customers if you provide better service than your competitors. It is important to remember that 9 out of 10 customers will turn to your competitor if they do not receive the treatment they deserve.

RESOURCE ALLOCATION AND PLANNING EFFECTIVELY

Allocating resources throughout your business in line with your business plan will ensure you meet your goals. Review your progress and identifies your growth strategy.

You may already have resources available or you may be able to generate them in the future to achieve one of your business goals. Before starting this process, it is critical to do some accurate budgeting before investing more cash in marketing, buying more equipment, or hiring more staff.

ENSURE YOUR WEB PRESENCE

Your website needs to meet your guests' demands, and in doing so, you need to develop a content strategy based on user behavior. Having a Website will increase your traffic and sales, but your content is more important than your design and programming.

A website offering products and services will also give you the opportunity to sell these on the web. It has the following advantages:

1. Reducing costs
2. Efficiencies and productivity are improved
3. It helps customers and suppliers communicate faster and more effectively
4. Your market reach can be easily expanded

AUTHENTICITY AND CONSISTENCY

It is important to foster the sense of trust between your business and your customers by being transparent, authentic, and consistent in all aspects of management. Consistency means staying true to your brand's values and messaging. Make sure you provide value to your customers and deliver on the promises you make to them. From the services you provide, the content you create, to how your business operates, make sure that you remain true to your brand message.

INCREASE YOUR FUNDING

In order to grow your business, extra funds are always needed. Among the easiest ways to get them are:

1. Offering shares to investors
2. Loans

Offering shares to investors
Determine how much the investment will increase your sales, if you're looking to add investors. Concentrate on how the sale will result in an increase in your business value.

Loans
Make sure your business can pay back the loan before you take it. Once you are sure you can pay it back, you can determine what loan you will take.

PROVIDE TRAINING TO YOUR EMPLOYEES

Providing training opportunities to your team will increase their loyalty and productivity, which will in turn increase your profits. Training yourself and your staff will help you improve the skills needed for your business

The key to ensuring your small business prospers is choosing a few ideas that are suitable for your business and circumstances and working towards growth. While growth may not be apparent immediately, keep at it. You will soon see improvements in your business.

Potency No. 710
is setting
their intentions
HIGHER.

TED

POTENCY
No. 710

When a skin care brand goes beyond beauty
a lifestyle is born. Potency is on a mission to elevate
skincare as a form of self care . Resulting in
maximum results and mindfulness.
Use code BUSINESS
to indulge in plant magic.

Potency710.com

POTENCY
No. 710®

HERE'S A LOOK AT 2022'S BEST-SELLING CARS, TRUCKS, AND SUVS

Subaru Outback

With new sales of the Subaru Outback 0.9 percent higher than last year, the Outback has maintained its sales level from last year. The crossover is popular because of Subaru's reputation.

Toyota Corolla

Despite this, the Toyota Corolla remains a perennial best-seller that saw its sales jump by 5 percent last year.

Honda Accord

Even though sedan sales are not as strong as they once were, there are still car enthusiasts who helped Honda increase Accord sales by 1.6 percent.

Hybrid and Hybrid EX-L scored 48 city/47 highway/47 total mpg. Hybrid Sport and Touring scored. Based on 2020 EPA mileage ratings, Hybrid Sport and Touring are rated 44 city/41 highway/43 combined. Driving conditions, battery age and condition, as well as how you maintain your vehicle, can influence your mileage.

HP total of the electric motors and gasoline engine as measured by their peak outputs at one time.

$26,120
STARTING

GMC SIERRA

SIERRA 1500 TRIMS

There's a Sierra 1500 that's perfect for any situation, no matter where you're headed or what you need to accomplish.

With a sophisticated, smart, and connected driving experience, Sierra offers features like available Super Cruise driver-assistance technologies with trailering and massive screens up to 14 CAMERA views. A stylish, luxurious interior that delivers authentic materials and first-class amenities that adds high-end comfort to even the roughest journeys.

Mazda CX-5

CX-5 crossover made Mazda's list of best-selling vehicles, despite competing in a highly competitive segment. However, CX-5 sales increased by 15 percent over.

Jeep Wrangler

Ford's new Bronco should not pose much of a threat to the Wrangler, which remains popular among enthusiasts. The venerable off-roader saw a 2 percent increase in sales in 2021-2022

Ford Explorer

Although its sales dropped, Ford Explorer remained a best-selling SUV IN 2021. It's time to explore with the Ford Explorer 2022. Comfortable and spacious, its interior can accommodate a large family. A connected build and athletic build make sure you make the most of every opportunity.
Starting at $33,745

BUSINESS INSIGHT
ELON MUSK
KING OF CRYPTO WORLD

BUSINESS INSIGHT
MARTHA STEWART

BUSINESS INSIGHT
RIHANNA
BECOMES A BILLIONAIRE
RICHEST FEMALE SINGER IN THE WORLD

BUSINESS INSIGHT
CHELSEA DONALDSON

BUSINESS INSIGHT
THE WILD SIDE OF BEAUTY

BUSINESS INSIGHT
KIM DAVIS
EMPOWER THE WOMEN, DEVELOP THE NATION!
7 Most Successful
Women Business Owners

BUSINESS INSIGHT
PERSONS OF THE YEAR
BUSINESS SUCCESS STORIES

BUSINESS INSIGHT
BUILD BACK BETTER IS
BECOMING WORSE AND
WORSE

BUSINESS INSIGHT
MARK WILLIAMS

ADVERTISING WITH
US CAN HELP YOUR
BUSINESS REACH
NEW HEIGHTS

FOR ADVERTISING

binsightmagazine@gmail.com
TEL: 214-256-4293

POTENCY
No. 710

POT GETS PERSONAL
MARIJUANA:
THE FUTURE OF
MEDICINE?
It's gaining popularity, but not everyone
agrees it helps what ails us.
BY CRAIG TOMASHOFF

THAT
MOMENT
YOU
REALIZE...

SELF
CARE
IS ESSENTIAL

POTENCY
No. 710

POTENCY710.COM

POTENCY
No. 710

Why You Need Cyber Threat Intelligence?

Analyzing data using tools and techniques is the process of providing meaningful information and insights regarding existing or emerging threats attacking the Businesses and assisting it in mitigating its risks. In order to combat threats, Businesses must become more proactive rather than reactive. Threat intelligence makes this possible.

The goal of cyber intelligence is to study threat data and provide information on adversaries in order to prevent or mitigate cyber-attacks. Through the provision of information on attackers, their motives, and capabilities, it can help identify, prepare, and prevent attacks.

Intelligence services provide valuable insights about these threats, help Businesses build effective defense mechanisms, and mitigate the risks that might negatively impact their finances and reputations. The purpose of Threat Intelligence is to proactively tailor the Businesses defenses and preempt future attacks for the future attacks they may encounter in the future.

As a security professional, a cyber threat analyst monitors and analyzes external cyber threat data. Researchers analyze data from different threat intelligence sources and analyze the pattern, methodology, motive, severity, and threat landscape of security incidents. After this data has been collected, it is analyzed and filtered accordingly to produce threat intelligence reports that help management (security officer) to take security-related decisions. Certified Threat Intelligence Analysts are usually the individuals who qualify for this position because they possess both knowledge and skills necessary for the job.

The Types of Threat Intelligence

Strategic Threat Intelligence

In strategic threat intelligence, a Businesses threat landscape is analyzed. It is less technical and designed primarily for high-level security professionals, who use the findings in the reports to drive strategic decision making.

Tactical Threat Intelligence

Intelligence on tactical threats is more specific details on threat actors' TTP and it is mainly for security teams to understand attack vectors and to build defensive strategies.

Technical Threat Intelligence

A technical threat intelligence analyst examines the indicators of compromise (IOCs), which include IP addresses, contents of phishing emails, malware samples, and fraudulent URLs to analyze attacks.

Operational Threat Intelligence

Specifically, operational threat intelligence provides insight into attack factors, such as motive, timing, and how the attack is conducted.

Challenges in gathering operational Intelligence:

- Communication between threats typically occurs through encrypted or private chat rooms, which are hard to access.
- The sheer amount of data in chat rooms or other communication channels makes it difficult for humans to gather relevant intelligence manually.
- Groups that threaten may speak in ambiguous and confusing ways to prevent anyone from understanding them

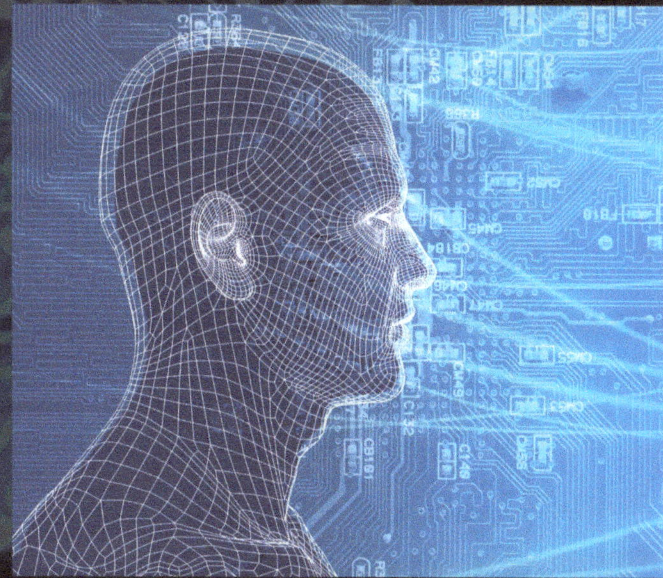

The following companies can provide Cyber Threat Intelligence for your business

http://www.sentinelone.com

http://www.exabeam.com

http://www.riskiq.com

BUSINESS INSIGHT
MAGAZINE | ISSUE 01
ELON MUSK
KING OF CRYPTO WORLD

BUSINESS INSIGHT
MAGAZINE | ISSUE 02
POTENCY 710
5 BEST CBD LUBES IN 2021
SEX AND THE CITY REBOOT
THE 30 MOST INFLUENTIAL WOMEN IN CBD INDUSTRY
MARTHA STEWART

BUSINESS INSIGHT
MAGAZINE | ISSUE 03
RIHANNA
BECOMES A BILLIONAIRE
RICHEST FEMALE SINGER IN THE WORLD

BUSINESS INSIGHT
MAGAZINE | ISSUE 04
CHELSEA DONALDSON
CEO OF PIVOTAL SOLUTIONS FOR YOUR HEALTH
EMPOWERING ENTREPRENEURS
EAT BETTER • LIVE BETTER • WORK SMARTER

BUSINESS INSIGHT
MAGAZINE | ISSUE 05
FACEBOOK WHISTLEBLOWER
WHAT IS HAPPENING INSIDE OF FACEBOOK?
THE WILD SIDE OF BEAUTY
FROM PETS TO PEOPLE FROM FOOD TO BEAUTY

BUSINESS INSIGHT
MAGAZINE | ISSUE 06
KIM DAVIS
Broker - Owner
EMPOWER THE WOMEN, DEVELOP THE NATION!
7 Most Successful Women Business Owners

BUSINESS INSIGHT
MAGAZINE | ISSUE 07
PERSONS OF THE YEAR
BUSINESS SUCCESS STORIES
ELON MUSK • KATHY MOTLAGH • DONALD TRUMP • JEFF BEZOS

BUSINESS INSIGHT
MAGAZINE | ISSUE 08
BUILD BACK BETTER IS BECOMING WORSE AND WORSE
ECONOMIC EXPERTS

BUSINESS INSIGHT
MAGAZINE | ISSUE 09
How to Make Your Small Business Thrive
Here's a look at 2022's best-selling cars, trucks, and SUVs
Why You Need Cyber Threat Intelligence?
MARK WILLIAMS
THE BATTLE OF A LIFETIME FOR AN EXECUTIVE
WHO'S SPENT A LIFETIME IN BUSINESS

INGLOT

ADVERTISING WITH US CAN HELP YOUR BUSINESS REACH NEW HEIGHTS

FOR ADVERTISING

binsightmagazine@gmail.com
TEL: 214-256-4293